Bud Collyer

WITH THE WHOLE HEART

FLEMING H. REVELL COMPANY
WESTWOOD • NEW JERSEY

Illustrations by Barry Martin

To Patricia, Cynthia, and Michael,
  who taught me so much
  that I needed to know.

PREFACE

These days everyone is looking for a gimmick—a twist to give a new meaning to an old thought. I frankly doubt if there is a single new idea among the old thoughts you will find in the pages of this book. But if anything expressed herein should give strength to the faint-hearted or courage to the half-hearted, if it should cause anyone to give himself or herself whole-heartedly to the work of the Lord, I shall be more than gratified!

BUD COLLYER

Contents

With the Whole Heart

I

Somebody has to do it! Why not you?
Someone always has to take the lead!
Too many seek to follow, while too few
Are willing to be counted when the need
For leadership has made its presence known
In every walk of life. We are so prone
To go along with those who criticize
By writing letters or by telephone

And adding still more voices to the cries
Which seek the abolition of those things
We once held dear in groups of human hearts
Gathered in bright and warm awakenings
To many truths, with many more false starts
Than any one of us would dare admit
Lest we might be accused of foolishness;
And yet we learn to make our actions fit
Comfortably within the restlessness
That stirs men's souls. We tried and found it
    good
To bind our hearts upon a common cause
And overcome what weaknesses we could
Until our growing strength soon gave us pause
To look around and survey where we stood
Before we strained to hear the crowd's applause!
Each group, no matter what its size, must find
A way to narrow down to one or two
Those who will give direction to mankind!
Somebody has to do it! Why not you?

The record that we live by is a proud one;
The errors in our judgment have been small.
The call for truth and honor is a loud one;
We've seen the haughty spirit take its fall!
So we must find within each other's striving

The echoes of the common good of man
And weave them all together, while contriving
Always to do the very best we can—
To build the better building for our dwelling,
To spin the finer gossamer to wear,
And truer tales to justify the telling—
With brighter landmarks shining everywhere!

What are the rules we live by in our growing?
What do we value as the greatest prize?
How do we face the many problems, knowing
Before we reach our goal we'll hear the cries
Of those whom guilty conscience brings to bear
Upon the weighted attitudes of man?—
And hearing them, perhaps we'll start to care
What happens to the purpose of God's plan!

Sometimes it seems too many years ago
That Jesus lived and walked this very earth.
Sometimes it seems it's not enough to know
That God was Jesus from His very birth!
Sometimes it seems that from our very youth
We ask so many questions on the way
From infant "doubt" to adolescent "truth,"
We face confusion! All too soon we pay

14

The price of pride's destruction; and the fee
Required by the devil's own demands
May rob us of our duty to be free
To keep the reins of truth within our hands!

A man came to see Jesus late one night
And said to Him, "We know You are a Teacher
Come from God with all the needed light
To show the way of love. You are a Preacher!
No one can do those things which you have done
Unless God be with him!" And Jesus said,
"Truly, I say to you—there is not one
To see the Kingdom as he is! Instead,
He must be born again!" And when some sought
To find out what He meant, He turned away,
Knowing the price with which they would be
      bought—
Knowing the price which He would have to pay.

We must be born again. What *does* this mean?
Does its significance lie in between
That which we do and that which we *must* do
Before we grasp the truth and see it through?
There is no shortcut and no other way
To stand before the Lord! Each one must pay

15

His own price of redemption! We must find
Our own supply of love and make it bind
Each heart to every other and release
Such truth that every will-to-war shall cease.
Then we must look within our lives and see
If we have lived each moment to be free,
Or if we moved too much in compromise
And wove a weary web of easy lies
Until the very fabric fell apart,
Exposing underneath the feeble heart
Of the *convenient* Christian—he who calls
Upon the Lord when troubled, but who falls
So easily beneath the simple spell
Of this world's magic. Only time can tell
How much rebirth is needed when we try
To use those well-known paths which you and I
Have always found to be good hiding places
For us to run and hide our many faces.
To be "reborn again" can simply mean
We must present our lives completely clean
Before the face of God! And to this end
We must make every enemy a friend!
We must do everything within our power
To plant the love of God in every hour!
We must achieve forgiveness by forgiving;

We must so cleanse our lives while we are living
Upon this earth that everyone will know,
No matter what we do or where we go,
That we have found our place beneath the cross,
Within whose shadow all that seemed like loss
Became the resurrected victory
As Jesus was reborn for you and me!

God loved the world so much He gave His Son—
His only Son—that all who may believe
And live a life of faith for everyone
Will have eternal life and will achieve
Awareness of the deeper, fuller sense
Church membership can have when we are part
Of Christ's own Body and in recompense,
We know the full forgiveness of His heart!

God sent His only Son to walk the earth
To save it, not to judge it; and the man
Who puts his faith in Him for all it's worth
And *lives* his faith in every way he can
Does not come under judgment. Only those
Who don't believe in Him and hate the light
Which shines between the cracks until it shows
Each unbeliever standing in God's sight—

These will be judged! All others will be saved
By faith in Jesus Christ, and there will be
Eternal life for everyone who braved
The heckling of the crowd and let them see
What strength God gives to all who turn His way
With the whole heart, to beat for Him alone!
What power over evil, come what may!
What joy and happiness when it is known
That any time the voice of Jesus calls,
Our answer will be swift and sure and true,
Catching a frightened heart before it falls
And breaks a dedicated life in two!

Once upon a time, a baby boy
Was born and made his father very proud!
He pleased his mother, too—and, in her joy
At bringing forth a man-child, she allowed
Her husband to take nearly all the credit!
He bragged of his "production" everywhere!
He said, "I made a son!" And when he said it,
He made one think his wife had not been there!
The child learned early, as all children do,
That just a little tear, a little smile,
Or just a certain look would see him through
Amazing situations, all the while

Quite conscious he was doing what he shouldn't,
Quite conscious he was naughty when he did it.
He did it when he could, but when he couldn't
He wrapped his conscience up before he hid it!
Each birthday and each Christmas was exciting,
As love translated fiction into fact.
To keep the flow of treasure without fighting
Became an endless travesty on tact!
Through grammar school, then high school, and
        then college
His doting underwriters paved the way,
Opening all the highest roads to knowledge
Whose final goal was graduation day!
If he then turned and bit the hand that fed him,
And, in his selfishness, if he became
Defiant of the very love that led him
To man's estate, on whom should fall the blame?
The story has so often been repeated
And in so very many different ways;
But every time some soul has been defeated
And started through the dark and angry days
That hurl defiance in the path of all
Who try to help and some who also seek
To circumvent the all-inclusive wall
Built around the things that make us weak.

For *man* so loves the world he gives his son,
Hoping that whosoever might believe
Will find the race worthwhile, and when it's done
Will find the way to gain a full reprieve,
Setting the son upon the upward way
Which leads to taking God down from the shelf
And hearing His reminder day by day
That each must love his neighbor as himself!
To love your neighbor you must first begin
By looking at yourself and then deciding
If what you see is really cutting thin
The difference between praising and deriding,
Of if the things you're doing in your living
From day to day are pleasing in your sight.
You must first love yourself, or else your giving
Of love to someone else will not be right.
I'm sure you realize I don't intend
To create the impression that "conceit"
And "vanity" are qualities that blend
Within the stream of life until they meet
And make a better person of their host,
Who treasures them as assets of his growing;
The braggart knows the subject of his boast!
The world knows, too, because his *self* is showing!
I simply mean Christ knew what He was saying

When He said, "Love thy neighbor *as thyself!*"
Recall the Pharisee who once was praying
And said, "I thank you, God, that I, myself,
Am not as other men!" Not far away
A tax-collector also prayed and said:
"Be merciful to me, O God, this day
For I'm a sinner!" And he bowed his head.
Which man do you think called the world his
     "brother"?
Which man could look his own life in the eye
And then bestow his self-love on another
And yet brush still another passing by?

In Switzerland two rivers come together
And join as one to roar down to the sea,
Like two great giants straining at a tether
And living for the moment to be free!
In one the water is so very blue,
So clean and white-capped as it flows along,
It brightens every town it passes through
And makes the things it feeds grow tall and strong!
The other river makes you stop and wonder
If such a thing can be—and so close by!
It looks as if the water flows down under
The biggest and the brownest mud supply

The world has ever known! And as they near
Their common meeting point, it seems a shame
The river which was once so blue and clear
Will soon have only history to blame
For its new face so full of mud and sand.
As the waters of the two begin to blend
Their contents, which will fall and which will
      stand
As victor when they come around the bend?
And now, for miles the single river twists
And turns its muddy way through town and city,
Hiding its dirty face in early mists
And memories when part of it was pretty.
Then something happens—and before your eyes
The murkiness begins to disappear,
And all the deep blue color of the skies
Comes back; and as you watch the water clear
It makes you realize just what took place
When Jesus calmly walked the ways of man
With just a gentle smile upon His face,
Knowing that when hollow lies began
To muddy up the waters of His life
He must not stop or even turn aside
From any scene of turbulence or strife,
But move ahead and never check His stride.

22

The evil that men do will cease to be
When Jesus mingles His life with another.
This is the only way for you and me—
To look upon a sinner as a brother!
The church of Jesus Christ has such a mission,
To carry out a campaign against sin;
Just as He died and 'rose for sin's remission,
So we must work and fight until we win!
For we are part and parcel of His Body;
We are all ministers of His living church,
Which summons, not just one, but everybody
To work with every other in the search
For the real truth that comes with sacrifice
As we join heartbeats with the "muddied streams"
That run into our lives—not once, but twice,
And even more—until it sometimes seems
We'll never breathe again the fresh, clean air
Which used to give us strength along the way;
But then we feel the love beyond compare
From deep within the church of Christ today!

Once there was a man who had a car.
Unfortunately this car had no wheels!
Obviously he could not go far.
And so, one day he rocked back on his heels

And made a big decision—he would trade
The engine from his auto with a friend
For four good wheels. He thought that he had made
A bargain which would bring soon to an end
His difficulties. Then he ascertained,
Without the motor it still would not run!
He hired a mechanic who was trained
With automotive knowledge by the ton!
He pointed out that with the motor missing
The car would never move. And so our man
Spent the next hour or so reminiscing
About his problems since he first began
To try to put his car in operation;
Then suddenly the light began to shine,
And standing out in this illumination
The basic fact, so logically in line
He wondered how he'd missed it from the start!
Each part of anything that's made for motion
Must help each other portion do its part
Before there's any forward locomotion.
So with our Christian church! It never "moves"
Unless each faithful Christian does his bit
As every opportunity improves
The chances for success. And if they fit
Too tightly in the frame, then try again

Until each part is part of every part,
Working together! Then, and only then,
Do we, as Christians, work *with the whole heart!*

For every one of us there is the choice
Of what part of Christ's Body we may be—
Perhaps the head, the heart, the hands, the voice—
Whatever talent lies in you and me.
For every one of us there is the chance
To serve as best we can in many ways
To bring about the strong and firm advance
Of Christian life throughout the future days.
For every one of us there are the means
Of doing what the Lord would have us do
To see that our direction always leans
Across the years from Calvary to you!
For every one of us there is the time
To turn the tide of evil into good—
Perhaps to turn ourselves and start the "climb"
With firm conviction, as a Christian should!
For every one of us there is the place
To use God's given love to truly heal
The illness of this world, with means of grace
To comprehend what Christian hearts reveal.
For every one of us the shining hour

When Jesus calls our name and takes our hand
And leads us to the greatest Source of Power,
Which only loving souls can understand!
For every one of us will have his turn
To prove what his wholeheartedness can do
To make the wheels of Christian doctrine turn.
Somebody has to do it! Why not you?

Plain and Solid Isometry

II

A young man by the name of Cyrus Field,
When he was very young and quite ambitious,
Determined he would make the future yield
A way to make the nations less suspicious
By bringing all their people close together.
With this in mind, he sought to interest others.
To find the way to break the ancient tether
Which held men back from reaching out as brothers

And made each group so separate and distinct
It grew within itself and fed upon
Its own ideals, making them so succinct
That he who ran could read and carry on
From generation on to generation;
Until there grew so much misunderstanding
As each group grew and soon became a nation
That men began to hunger for the landing
Of *any* pilgrim's feet on *any* rock,
If only they would feed the hungry heart
By putting down some roots and taking stock
Of where to build a home and how to start.
Notice I said a *home* and not a *house*—
Both will give shelter, both will keep you warm,
Both are havens to a man or a mouse,
Both can be the place you're safe from harm.
But only one can be the place for living
Where loving is the order of each day,
And only one can understand forgiving
When any human fault gets in the way.
Only a home can live for each tomorrow
As if there never was a day before,
Bringing a love to banish any sorrow
And leaving some for all who ask for more.

30

And so a home springs in another land,
With yet another's different way of speech
And still another's gentle touch of hand,
As each starts to communicate with each.
It's always worth the effort that is made,
Regardless of the pain or of the cost;
It doesn't have the time to be afraid,
And if it's won with love, it's never lost!

The youth I mentioned tried to find a way
To stretch a cable on the ocean floor
And so he spent his every waking day
Seeking some help to open up the door
To faith and confidence of other men
In what he planned to do; and if he found
They turned the other way, he tried again,
Until he proved his theories were sound.
He raised some money, and the work began,
Through days and nights
    that seemed to have no end,
While trial and error tested every plan
To make of every enemy a friend.
This cable would enable men to speak
Across the broad Atlantic to each other
And so communicate, and every week
Exchange ideas and plans with one another.

An ocean-going trawler put to sea
With miles and miles of cable in its hold.
The miles they put behind them were but three
When something happened in the bitter cold,
And they were forced to start the job again.
Our hero had spent most of his own money,
And yet, despite the heartache and the pain,
He managed, with the weather warm and sunny,
To try his luck once more. They started out
With the same boat, loaded with fresh supplies.
Before they knew what it was all about,
And right before their disappointed eyes,
The cable snapped, and they were forced to quit
And turn the ship around and head for port.
His friends all urged him to have done with it
And seek a future of a different sort.
Try as they would, he could not be dissuaded,
But merely took a breath and started out
To find some others who could be persuaded
To have the kind of faith that knows no doubt,
But takes a chance on courage, and good sense,
And willingness to share another's dream
By underwriting every new expense
And lighting one star by another's gleam!

Five times he tried within the next few years—
Five times he failed to make his dream come true,
Five times he saw his ever-growing fears
Confront a task too difficult to do!
But on his sixth attempt he found success!
His cable joined the new world with the old.
In spite of every hardship and duress,
In spite of summer's heat and winter's cold,
In spite of lack of confidence and cash,
In spite of loss of friends and loss of face,
In spite of seeing his ambitions crash,
He managed to face up to each disgrace
And try once more! I'm sure we realize
Just what it takes to reach a distant dream—
How many times it falls before our eyes
Before we gain the service of a team
Which brings its own belief in what we do,
And all the spark to make a plan succeed,
And all the faith to make a dream come true,
And all the wherewithal to fill a need!

Today we take for granted all the wires
And cables which are sent around the world,
Robbing all secrets of their hidden fires

34

And picking up all gauntlets that are hurled
Across the face of men too scared to be
The heroes which are needed on the stage
Where man works out his anxious destiny,
And writes his name on history's trembling page!

Just recently I met a friend of mine
From whom I had not heard for several years.
I asked him how he was; and he said "fine,"
But that he'd had his share of doubts and fears,
And could we go somewhere and have a talk.
I, of course, agreed—and then he told
Of how, three years before, he took a walk
To clear his mind and make his path unfold
So he might see just where his steps were leading
Before he tripped and fell upon his face,
Hating to admit that he was feeding
His vanity upon his own disgrace!
He had become a drunkard when he lost
His only son of barely twenty-three;
And for two years he couldn't count the cost
In loving friends who tried to set him free
And make him see that he had cut the lines
Of all communication to his heart.
He could no longer see nor hear the signs

Which might have shown the place
     where he must start
To make the long climb back. He didn't care
What might become of him. He turned away
From everyone! He said he'd stand and stare
At each young face that passed him every day
And try to fit them all into a dream
In which he found his son alive again.
This took his tragic loss and made it seem
As though he'd never felt the awful pain.
His son had helped to fight a forest fire
That threatened to destroy their home. He tried
So hard he failed to see the fallen wire.
He tripped—and fell into the flames—and died!
My friend, of course, blamed God. He couldn't see
Why God should do a thing like that to him!
Why pick on him and let the rest go free,
Leaving him victim of a Godly whim?
He'd gone about as far as he could go
When two or three friends gathered in God's name;
And they were blessed with love,
     so they could throw
All caution to the winds and take what blame
My friend might lay to them, until he saw
How patiently and lovingly they tried

To lift him up again. His nerves were raw—
He screamed against them all—until he cried.
He sobbed his agony for all to hear;
He never even heard the things they said
To try to help him throw aside his fear
And reach to grasp the hand of God instead.
Then, deep within him, came a voice so strong,
So calm, it made him listen for his heart,
For fear it might have stopped! It wasn't long
Before he understood the words. In part,
They said, "You are My son—My well-loved son
In whom I would be pleased if you would let Me.
You closed your mind, and as you turned to run
You made a firm resolve that you'd forget Me.
But every time you tried, your loving friends
Would bring you back, so that you had to face Me;
And every time they tried to make amends,
You used your finest efforts to disgrace Me.
I'll talk with you if you will talk with Me,
And maybe we can find a common place
Where truth will shine again, and you will see
The answers as you look upon My face."

This is all my friend remembers now
As he looks back upon the last three years.

He doesn't claim to understand just how
He made the long climb back beyond his fears.
He only knows he's dearly loved by others
Who gave themselves to help him find the way.
He knows the world is filled
         with just his brothers;
He knows each dawn will bring a brighter day.

The world once had one language and few words.
In Shinar all men settled on a plain.
They split their crowded numbers into thirds
And planned to build a tower to explain
How man might climb to God and seize His throne.
God heard, and He came down to take a look
At what His creatures planned. He stood
         alone,
As many times He would before His Book
Was ever written, and He shook His head
At what He saw. He knew what He must do—
He must confound their language, and, instead
Of having only one or even two,
All of them must be scattered, so that each
Lived in a different place, a different land.
They'd have no knowledge of each other's speech,
And, even though they tried to understand,

They'd be confused. And so man lost the way
For prompt communication with his brother.
And ever since that time, try as they may,
Men never fully understood each other.
The need for understanding is acute
In our imperiled world. There is such need
To cut through lies and half-truths and refute
All twisting of the truth in word and deed.
Science and inventiveness are King,
With strength for peace determined just by power,
With atom-might the most important thing—
These are the bricks
      with which we build our tower—
Hoping with our own knowledge we may see
What makes our Father-God-Creator tick,
Hoping that when He looks at you and me
We'll learn that all creation is a trick
That we can do ourselves; for, after all,
We've done quite well so far—and on our own—
We've split the atom—made a bomb to fall—
And soon, perhaps—one man will stand alone—
And how alone!! No single soul to turn to—
No language barrier then—no one to speak to!
No children and no living wife to yearn to!
Not even one, small, frightened mouse to squeak to!

39

No one at all!! No single living thing!!
Do you think *then* he'll turn to God and say,
"You are my God, Creator, Father, King!
Forgive me, God, and help me find my way!"
Might God then look upon him with a frown
And say, "May I remind you, I once said
Where *two* or *three* are gathered, I'd look down
And bless them! But you come to Me instead
As only *one*, and you ask Me to take you
And wipe away all fear, all doubt, all dread,
And then, as from a nightmare, gently wake you!
I tried so hard to build an understanding
That men might reach each other through *My* heart,
And give each flight of love a happy landing.
But no! You sought to tear the world apart
And build on hate and greed and jealousy,
Raising your tower of power, whose first brick
Would one day fall apart so you might see
That My creation isn't just a trick!
But come—I'll take you in and start again
To build a better species than before.
Perhaps I'll even have to come again
To prove at last what love is really for!"

There are eternal principles of God

Which cannot be defied by any man,
And anyone who digs beneath the sod
Of man's behavior patterns finds the plan
By which God seeks to set His children free
So they may soar to greater heights above,
So *you* may learn to talk *through* God to *me*,
And find the light of everlasting love!
A common language of the human soul
Will be recovered only when men learn
That their own "bricks" can only fill a hole.
It takes the love of God to make the turn
Within our lives to prove to one and all
That Jesus Christ once lived and died—and *lives!*
And everyone who answers to His call
Will know He lives and loves—and He forgives!

All right, you youth, you young ones,
        here's your chance!
You think you know the answers, one and all!
You never seem to need a second glance
To know when life is backed against the wall!
You're pretty sure we older ones have had it
And that we've blundered far more than we've
        scored.
You take the measure of our sins and add it

And find results that really have you floored!
You wonder how the world and you could stand us
As we came stumbling down the road of life.
No wonder the psychiatrists could land us
And find us somewhat duller than a knife!
And yet, before too many years have passed you,
You'll find that your position is reversed—
And younger youths have grown up and
    out-massed you,
And *you* are second-string and *they* are first!
I hope before that time that you may learn
How much all generations need each other—
How much Age needs the Youthful heart to burn
With eagerness to call the world his "brother";
How much Youth needs the calmness of the Older
To stabilize his eager, headlong flight,
And still to put his steady, heady shoulder
Behind the wheel that turns from "wrong"
    to "right"!
Somewhere we seem to lose communication
And fail to turn to God to help us out.
Somewhere we lose the real determination
To speak without the shadow of a doubt!
So there's a job for youth—find out the reason
We all can't speak one language as we should,
Why we can't get across in any season

The things we *could* do if we only *would*!
So take the will to do it, and you'll *do* it!
Both teach and learn to speak another way!
If you need strength to help,
    we'll see you through it,
And very soon we'll find that sun-filled day
When generation talks to generation,
Each hearing what the other has to say,
Each resting with a calm determination
Within the heart of God—and day by day
We'll find we know just what the other's saying
Without a single shadow of a doubt!
We'll find communication just by praying
And never let God's fire of love go out!

A plain and simple fact of life today
Involves an isometric exercise
To keep yourself from growing old and grey
And getting senile right before your eyes.
It does seem strange,
    the ones who have the strength—
The youthful ones with their vitality—
Should be the ones to go to any length
To save their mortal immortality,
Inventing exercises to be done
In less than half the time it used to take,

With far less effort and with much more fun
And greater benefits for each one's sake.
Somehow the *spirit* doesn't *grow* this way;
It needs the challenge and the effort, too!
It needs the "pilgrim's progress," day by day—
It needs the work put forth by me and you!
There is no short-cut in communication;
Just reach out to your neighbor everywhere.
The antidote for sheer procrastination—
Wherever you search for God
     you'll find Him there!
If isometric exercises aid you
To find a simple way to instant health,
While working nine to five has amply paid you
To find a quicker way to instant wealth,
Remember that your spirit may be starving—
There's nothing isometric for your soul.
So talk a lot with God, and you'll be carving
A brand new road, with Jesus as its Goal!
We'll shout directions out, because we've seen them
When we passed by so very long ago.
We'll need your youth to push our way between
     them
And help us through the trials we'll undergo!
Let's never fail to talk with one another!

Through God let's send what we don't understand.
He'll help us talk quite clearly with each other
If we just hold our Father by the hand!

This Above All

III

Remember when you sat upon the knee
Of someone bigger than yourself—your Dad?
Remember how this contact set you free
From all the fear and nervousness you had
Whenever things went wrong with some pet plan
You started with your brain and let your heart
Surround it with the trappings of a man
Until its own weight made it fall apart?

Remember how you held each broken piece
And tried to make it stick against its "brother"
With just the glue of tears, which wouldn't cease
Without the love and friendship of another—
Your father! What a hero! What a guy!
How handsome and how brave he was! How tall!
The only one who'd never pass you by,
But helped you up each time he saw you fall!
How precious is the legendary hero
Who steps in when the blackest fears are mounting,
Smiles at a worth that's something less than zero,
And finds a value that defies accounting!

We live within a time whose "witching hour"
Seems to be all around us all the time,
Making dark the tallest ivory tower
To which each frightened man-child seeks to climb!
Every creature seeks its own protection
Where danger casts a shadow in its way!
Sometimes a bigger stone, a new direction,
Will cause the heart to beat for one more day!
And always when the peril seems the gravest,
Without a single hope for our salvation,
Somehow the finger falls upon the bravest
To step forth from the crowd and lead a nation
Back from the precipice that falls to fear,

Back from the edge of darkness into light,
Back to those high ideals once held so dear,
Back to the day which always follows night!
Every deep emotion of the soul—
Whether it be malice, fear, or hate,
Or greed, or envy at another's role,
Or deep resentment that another's fate
Seems to surpass the fortunes of the day
And brings to pass such turnings of the wheel
That, where one seems to stumble on the way,
Another holds the course and seems to feel
Contempt for any weakness—each emotion,
Even when its birthplace is the brain,
Must reach the heart to find the magic potion
On which it feeds! And if it can obtain
Complete control of its whole human host,
Then such a force of evil is released
It seems to justify the wildest boast,
And turns immortal man to mortal beast!
But don't forget—within the cruelest heart
There lies the same capacity for love;
It only takes the simplest thing to start—
A gentle push from God—a quiet shove
Out of the swirling eddies of the tide,
Out of the rocks that crash another's dream
Within whose grasp a million plans have died,

And into the conscious current of the stream,
Whose deepest pools are mirrors which reflect
The truth of all that passes overhead,
Giving us pause to reason and reject
Those things which are impure, and in their stead
To cause such good and proper things to grow
That life becomes what it should always be—
The answer to all things we seek to know
Within the love of God for you and me!
How thrilled the world became when it was told
The atom had been smashed! Here was the thing
Once called the smallest that the mind could hold!
Now any of its simplest parts could bring
Such power and such monumental force
As to defy the full imagination
And push all former knowledge from the course,
Into the scientific consternation
Of all the keenest brains! What new direction
Would now be taken in the search for peace?
Was this the thing to use for our protection,
Confident that the urge for war would cease?
Could it be so controlled that it would serve
The cause of man's *humanity* to man?
Or would we be afraid and lose our nerve
And see the formulation of a plan
Whose only merit is a compromise

To check the great impertinence of man
And bring the kind of peace which terror buys!
Although we try to do the best we can,
With so much fear pervading all we do
And so much doubt invading every thought,
What guidelines can be found for me and you—
What strength to help us do the things we ought?

Approximately four short years ago
A woman, having trouble with her vision,
Decided it was time for her to know
Just what the future held. With this decision
She called upon her doctor for advice;
He checked her eyes—and then he gently said,
"There's nothing to be done, at any price!"
"Not anything?" she cried. He shook his head:
"Your sight will go! There's nothing I can do!"
Fear grabbed at her—but missed!
      Within her breast
She thought: "At least there's something *I* can do—
While I have sight I'll study all the best
In everything around me—and I'll learn
To reach my hand into the hands of others
And learn to serve at each and every turn,
Bringing me close to all who are my brothers

Throughout this whole wide world! And while
    I see
I'll take my Bible from its dusty shelf
And take each golden opportunity
To learn to love my neighbor as myself!"
Month after month went slipping by; and yet
Her sight, while growing dimmer, still remained.
She still could see to serve, and pay the debt
She felt she owed to God. She worked and strained
With every ounce of energy she had
To find each need, and, be it large or small
Or be the needy person good or bad,
She somehow always seemed to stop the fall.
She told her friends, "If my capacity
For love and friendship can remain as big
When I am blind as now while I can see,
Then I'll have the ability to dig
The darkness out of all the darkest days
And let the brightest reaches of my soul
Illuminate my efforts, while each phrase
I bring to bear upon the farthest goal
Will speak so clearly to the weakest ear
That every whisper will be worth the labor
And I will touch all hearts, both far and near,
While finding that the whole world is my
    neighbor!"

This is the kind of channel that God seeks
To do His work and let His will be known!
This is the kind of voice through which God speaks
To tell us we shall never be alone!

The woman of our story isn't blind;
Her sight, while never perfect, still improves!
She left the guess of experts far behind
And showed the wondrous way in which God
    moves!
God's love has always moved in three directions—
The first one is from Him to you and me,
Reaching in our lives to make corrections
In every feeble fault His eye can see!
The second is from us to Him, and here
Our selfishness is often in the way!
The third one is the one God holds most dear
And gives the greatest challenge every day—
From one man to another! You'll recall
The story of a certain businessman.
En route to Jericho he chanced to fall
Into the hands of robbers, who began
To rob him and to beat him 'til he dropped—
They then departed, leaving him half dead!
It happened that a priest came by. He stopped,
He looked, and thought of helping, but instead

56

He hurried past. In just a little while
Another man, a Levite, came along,
Having traveled many a weary mile.
His pack was on his donkey; he was strong—
He could have lifted up the dying man
And carried him to shelter on his way.
He had a chance for service—but he ran
Across the road and left him where he lay!
Then came a strange Samaritan. His beast
Was burdened with his articles of trade.
He bound the man's wounds till all bleeding
    ceased,
Then took him to an inn, and there he paid
All the expense of lodging for the night.
He could have stopped at this—but he went on
And told the innkeeper about the plight
Of his new guest—how he'd been set upon
By robbers and then left alone to die.
He told him that he'd gladly pay the bill
For all the stranger's needs when he came by
On his return trip!
              Call it what you will—
Compassion or concern or charity—
This was the love that brings eternal living,
This was the love that helps the heart to see,
This was the love you only get through giving!

And this, in serving God, is what you do!
This is the open heart which always speaks
Each time the chance for service channels through
And finds the kind of willingness it seeks!

With all the panic Communism brings
And with mankind so anxious to be safe,
With even Red-ruled countries doing things
Among their own Red rulers—things that chafe
And irritate themselves within themselves,
Until each frantic effort to deny it
Causes each to reach to Marxist shelves
To find old reasons why the world should try it,
What reasons do we have for all our worry?
Let's give it all the freedom it can use!
What reasons do we have for all our hurry
To top them in the arms-race? We confuse
And soon confound ourselves as they are doing,
With only gods of matter for their might!
We have a God *who matters*, still pursuing
Each one of us through every day and night,
And trying hard to make us all be still
And *know* that He is God! If we just trust
And let Him do the things He can and will,
While Communism falters, as it must

When it's brought face to face
      with all that's true,
There will be time within that time to reach
Each brain-washed soul, to lead them gently
      through
From red to white, and then begin to teach
By what we do that there are better ways
To know the joys mere living can contain.
Through service to each other we can gaze
Down the great throughway to the greater gain,
And from each move the heroes will step out
To take us in their strong and steady hands
And lead us into faith which knows no doubt,
Where every "doubting Thomas" understands!

For all who serve the Lord there come the chances
To live a life of service every day;
For each of you the seldom backward glances
Will show the good you've done along the way.
For each of you there'll always be the blind ones
Who need your sturdy steps to guide their feet;
For each of you, the chance to be the kind ones
Who fill the gaps and make all life complete;
For each of you, the time to make your living
The heartbeat of the nearest dying soul;
For each of you, the means to be forgiving

While counting up the wealth another stole;
For each of you, the clean and happy knowledge
That lights the way along the darkest road;
For each of you who sees a child through college,
The chance to teach to share another's load;
For each of you,
      when all your friends are frightened
By every evil force that threatens death,
The chance to see another's burden lightened
With courage from your own eternal breath!

The First Will

IV

A scant, short week each year we've celebrated
A day which nearly all of us have rated
As one which stands out from among the rest;
And every year the world is quite impressed
By what good Christians do. Our big "parade,"
Which represents the price that has been paid
For every Easter bonnet, every dress
Purchased under husbandly duress,

Shows to all who care to look our way
That we know how to celebrate this day.
Of course, deep down within our hearts we know
The day is more than just a fashion show!
We're well aware that most of it is habit
And that the deeper meaning is a rabbit!
But wait! There's something else!
      Oh, yes, the church—
Where we could gather and pursue the search
Through empty tombs where stones were rolled
    away,
Proclaiming to the world that on this day
Eternity was opened to mankind!
To love God with all heart and soul and mind
Is all we have to do! If this command
Were carried out each day throughout the land,
No longer would we know the sound of fear,
Which deafens us until we cannot hear
The voice of Jesus calling from the cross,
And changing what had seemed like total loss
To profit such as none had ever known,
And promising that none shall be alone
Who puts his faith in Jesus!
                  Deep within
Each one of us, a tiny pricking pin
Called "conscience" makes us look within our souls

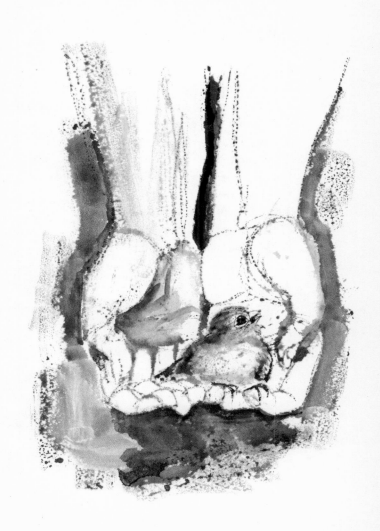

To see if we have set the proper goals,
Enabling us to share the bread and wine
With Jesus and to take our place in line
And see again the very empty grave
Proclaiming to the world: "He died to save!"

I wonder if it ever has occurred
To any one of us, when we have heard
The name of Judas talked about with scorn,
That from the very day when we were born
There always was the possibility
That each of us might one day fail to see
Beyond the gleam of silver or of gold,
Until we realize that we have sold
The very precious birthright of a brother,
Condoning the betrayal of another.
Satan, the worldly prince, by any name
Would smell as evil as the day he came
To make God's creatures all too well aware
Of power, greed, and envy; and to care
So much for all material things on earth,
We sell the very reason for our birth.

Can you imagine what it must have meant
Two thousand years ago to be alive
And working hard, while trying to present

A halfway good appearance, and to strive
With half-a-heart to better what you do,
Wondering the while if there would be
A good meal and a good night's rest for you;
And when the day was over, possibly
A bit of fun within a group of friends,
A chance to laugh and sing a bit of song,
Or maybe take the time to make amends
For what you'd call imaginary wrong.
And then, when morning brought another day,
It also brought a strange and gentle man,
Who called to you as you went on your way
To carry out your daily working plan.
He smiled—and you smiled back—and as you tried
To pass Him by, He gently touched your arm
And said, "Come! Follow Me!" And by His side
Were several other men, whose smiles were warm
And friendly; and they made you feel so good,
It never once occurred to you to say,
"I'm sorry, but I have to get some food
To feed my family through another day!"
He just said, "Follow Me!" But in His voice
Something made your very breath stand still,
Something made your inner heart rejoice,
Something made you long to drink your fill
Of everything this simple Man might give

And long to give back something in return.
You knew that He could teach you how to live;
You knew that He could teach you how to earn
A way of life you'd never known before.
You had no way to tell when you began
To follow Him what hardships were in store,
What testing and what trials were in God's plan;
And so you went along, and through the days
In which you heard Him teach and saw Him heal,
And saw both truth and love within His gaze,
And felt the growing pull of His appeal,
Suddenly it was a different world!
Suddenly it was a richer life!
Suddenly the future was unfurled!
Suddenly, for every man and wife,
For every child, for every living thing,
There came such keen awareness of His fate,
As selfish men would seek to make Him king,
It was too late to back out, much too late!
You'd learned to love this Jesus, and to be
Amazed at how He handled each device
By which men sought to trap Him, and to see
How well He knew He'd have to pay a price
To buy back all of mankind's wasted losses,
Redeem man from his sins, and make amends;
Yet see ahead a hill that held three crosses

And faces in a crowd that held no friends!
You saw Him make so little feed so many.
You saw one blind from birth regain his sight.
You heard Him praise the widow with her penny.
You watched Him make all dark things seem so
     bright.
You watched Him raising Lazarus from the dead.
You saw the cripple leave his bed and walk.
And you began to sense what lay ahead—
You heard the mutterings—you heard the talk—
As well-placed rabble-rousers had their say
And pointed Jesus toward His greatest day!

And then—that last night in the upper room—
Twelve troubled hearts and One who knew His
     fate,
Like many fragments weaving through a loom
Designing things which only men create.

"One of you shall betray Me!"

                                    What a shock
Would have raced through your mind if you'd
     been there!
What stunned surprise, as everyone took stock
And wondered which one of the twelve would dare
Betray the Son of Man, who loved them so

He shared His life and called each one His friend!
And when the one among them turned to go
To set in motion forces which would rend
The temple veil—could you have been that man?
Could you have greeted Jesus with a kiss
When it was part and parcel of a plan
To hand Him to His enemies? Is this
Something you're sure that you would never do?
Perhaps you'd be the first one to protest
And swear to all that it could not be you.
Perhaps you might stand out among the rest,
Like Peter, strong and forthright, as he said,
"I'll gladly give my life for You, my Lord!"
But Jesus gently shook His weary head
And answered: "Do not say another word
For which you may be sorry, for before
The cock crows and we know another day,
You'll have at least three chances, maybe more,
To prove that you will give your life away
For Me; for some will ask if you are one
Of My good friends who walked the way with Me.
Three times you'll answer 'no'! And when it's done
You'll hear the rooster crowing, and you'll see
That life is very precious to mankind,
And if you lay it down for any other,
You'll know that I am with you, and you'll find

The joy of bringing real love to a brother!"

Then, knowing what the next few hours would
        bring,
Jesus looked around Him at the men,
Who hoped in secret hearts that He'd be king
And merely wondered how and where and when
The coronation would take place. They tried
To understand the things He said to them,
But they would never know until He died
Why those whom they were eager to condemn
He ordered them to love and to forgive;
For only in this way could all mankind
Overcome the sting of death and live
Forever, leaving fear and doubt behind,
And, moving onward through eternity,
Hear all the things they never thought they'd hear
And see the things they never thought they'd see.
So Jesus looked at those He held most dear.
He tried to think of something He might say
To drive the dreary dark of doubt away.
He saw their faces filled with doubt and fright,
He heard their whispered questions, and He tried
To think of all the things to say that night
And what to leave to them before He died!
He had no property of any worth,

71

No money, and no goods of any kind,
No place to call His anywhere on earth;
And yet the will He made, the will He signed
With His own blood and with His wounded hand,
Was something everyone could understand.
The first will! The first Christian will of all!
"Peace I leave with you," He said. "My peace
I give to you!" And all who heard that call
Felt every hidden fear and worry cease!
"Not as the world gives do I give to you!
Let not your hearts be troubled or afraid!
You know that there are things that I must do;
You know there is a price which must be paid!
I go away, but I'll come back to you!"

What we call the "last will and testament,"
By which we seek to leave a legacy,
Hoping our heirs will know just what we meant,
In this case was a "first will"! We can see
Within the heart of Jesus, as He faced
The anguished hours ahead! He must have thought,
How could He let these moments go to waste,
These rushing, racing moments which had caught
The lives of twelve disciples with His own,
And not do what He could to give them strength
And make them understand there'd be no throne,

But merely threats and lies, until at length
All passion and all agony would cease;
He left behind the first great Christian will—
His own God-given legacy of peace,
The freely given peace of God, which still
Presents to all of us alive today
And living in anxiety and doubt
The answer to it all, the only way
To see the truth and bring it all about!

Back in the nineteen-twenties we were thrilled
To hear how some explorers had discovered
The tomb of an Egyptian, which was filled
With treasures such as no one had uncovered
Ever before. This ancient burial place,
Protected from the ravages of time
By deeper burial, had not left a trace
To be discerned by any who might climb
To higher places to dig other graves,
Causing great piles of small rock chips to slide
And make the kind of covering which saves
Everything the old Egyptians tried
To save and to preserve forevermore.
They mummified the bodies in a way
That made them look much as they did before,
When they were full of life; and to this day

73

Their ancient, secret methods are not known
To modern scientists, who try their best
To duplicate a skill which had been shown
To be an art which had endured the test
Of temperature, humidity, and years
Which raced along so rapidly, the most
A man could do was register his fears
And hope the gods would let him reach the coast
Of life in a hereafter which was filled
With need for things he needed when alive.
So when his heartbeat finally was stilled,
With what was buried with him he could thrive!
The ancient grave we speak of here belonged
To Tutankhamen, Pharaoh of the Nile,
And scientists of many nations thronged
Around the tomb, with its impressive pile
Of works of art in ivory and gold
And precious stones to decorate the king
As any future journey might unfold,
So he would never lack for anything.
King Tut was still a young lad when he died
And had his body buried with his treasures;
He hoped to take them to the "other side"
To pay the cost of his post-mortem pleasures.
Today, inside an ornate mummy case
His dried remains remain for all to see,

Trapped within a musty, airless place,
Without a single god to set him free.

Our friends in Moscow also have a tomb.
It really is a most impressive room;
And inside is a most impressive guest,
Expressing Communism at its best.
He's dead! And yet his body seems alive
And just asleep. It really seems to thrive
On the long lines of comrades who believe
That from his mummied presence they receive
The strength they need to last another year
Of living under tyranny and fear.
So Lenin lies, and Communism lies,
For truth cannot be seen by godless eyes!

Time now to look within another grave
To see what treasures we can find to save
For future generations. We can stare
At our own Christian "mummy." We can share
As fine a shrine as any of the rest!
In all the world we'll have the very best!
But wait! Our tomb is empty! Can it be
We'll be denied the opportunity
Of other men to stand in line and stare?
Why is our shrine so empty and so bare?

Good Christians, thank God for this empty place
Filled to the top with all the means of grace
God grants to those who know what happened
    here!
Here was the birth of faith, the death of fear!
Empty of everything that smells of death!
Filled with the life that comes
    from God's own breath!
No corpse! No body! Jesus resurrected!
Down from the cross which frightened men erected,
Back to His life of loving and forgiving
To prove to doubters He is really living.
Sharing a meal with just a chosen few!
Walking a road with some until they knew!

It's true our tomb is empty of the dead.
No corpses can be found inside; instead,
It's full of life and all that is alive
And all that lives in faith and will survive
Beyond the end of time's eternity,
Until the day when everyone shall see
That God is love and God is all that's true,
And God is all that's old and all that's new!
In the very beginning was the Word,
And the Word became flesh, and is our risen Lord!
Today we move so fast, with all our going

And coming through the simple doors of living,
We're far too prone to miss the means of knowing
The way to ask forgiveness while forgiving.
We're apt to miss the simple little things
That point the perfect way to happiness;
And, in our climb from "cabbages to kings,"
Overlook the path to real success.
Yet every time we take one little hour
To listen to the heartbreak of a friend,
And every time we grow one little flower
To say we're sorry when we might offend,
And every time we smile a little brighter
To bring some gladness to a tragic way,
And every time our laugh's a little lighter
To bring some sunshine to a gloomy day,
And every time we stop to ease an illness
To comfort someone's suffering and pain,
And every time we break into a stillness
To sing a hymn and wipe away a stain,
And every time we consecrate a minute
To faith that makes an ailing body heal,
And every time we take the seconds in it
To teach the numbest doubter how to feel,
And every time we realize our duty
To offer our lives in another's stead,
And every time we show the truth of beauty

To those who see just ugliness ahead,
And every time we join the happy chorus
Of Christians singing so the world can hear,
It makes the sky a little clearer for us,
And brings our Lord of love so very near!
Within each one of us there come those times
When fears take over every worried thought,
When panic digs its clawing feet and climbs
To such great heights you'd think we'd never
    fought
A single fight with courage in our eyes,
And, having only cowardice to guide us,
Trusting only in a pack of lies
To cover us completely and to hide us!
The world today is filled with so much fear
It's difficult to sort out what you hear
Into neat piles of truths, half-truths, and lies,
To turn Time's face around, and in its eyes
Find the facts which don't equivocate
And leave you unprepared to meet your fate!
It's difficult! But that must never mean
That it's impossible, for in between
The lines there is much reading to be done
To point the way before the race is won;
And in such reading you will always see
The rich reward in Jesus' legacy!

The One who paid the one redeeming cost
And set us free when everything seemed lost
Has given to us all the greater power
The world has ever known; and in that hour
When everything seems darkest, use your heart
To open up God's Christian will and start
The long pull up the hill to victory,
Holding a banner everyone can see—
An empty cross to tell of Jesus' death,
An empty tomb to tell of His new breath!

"Rejoice in the Lord always; again I say
Rejoice!" Let all men know each time you pray
That Jesus is at hand; so let your fears
Pass quickly down the ever-moving years
Until they move beyond the great white light
And disappear in never-ending night!
Believe in God the Father! God the Son!
Believe! And let His holy will be done!

What Have We Got
to Live For?

V

What have we got to live for, you and I?
What is there worth one tick of memory's clock
To motivate our reaching to the sky?
Why do we fail to hear the steady knock
Upon the door of every human heart
That tells us there is One who waits outside,
Where He has waited since the very start
Of everything that leads to mortal pride?

The threat of man's destruction of himself
And all the many things he holds most dear
Must cause a rearrangement of the shelf
Which keeps his thoughts beyond the reach of fear!
What happened to the happiness and joy,
The promise of fulfillment that we knew
When every challenge was another toy
To play with, while our fears were very few
And far between? Was this another life,
Another place in time, another name
For what we now call fortune? Could a knife
Slide between our constant quest for fame
And separate our bodies from our souls
While walking on the narrow edge of dread,
Digging in our heels and making holes
To cover up our sins when we are dead?

When God created us He set us free
To live and love and even to beget,
To smell, to taste, to listen, and to see,
To understand so many things, and yet
We fail to even start to comprehend
What we must do with all these gifts of power,
Where we must go before we reach the end
And gently wither like a lovely flower.

Just as all other forms of life reach out
To touch each other as they quickly pass,
Just so must we, without a single doubt,
Reach beyond the darkness of the glass
Until we see each other face to face,
Until the things which now we know in part
Bring us closer to the means of grace
To know as we are known in God's own heart!

Once upon a long, long time ago,
A sabbath dawned, like any other day.
There seemed no way for anyone to know
That Jesus' life would find another way
To move just one step closer to the cross—
To give the Pharisees another chance
To try to load the dice and win the toss,
Hoping that with a nod or with a glance
He'd break a law or do a sinful thing,
Or say a word which they might label "treason,"
Just as today we try so hard to bring
So much that's false within the name of reason!
Within the crowd that pressed so close about Him
A man who had a withered hand came near—
He had no cause to trust Him or to doubt Him.
When Jesus softly said to him, "Come here!
Stretch out your arm!" he did so—and his hand

Became as strong and healthy as the other;
And no one in the crowd could understand—
They merely stood and looked at one another.
But not the Pharisees! This was their chance!
One of them said, "This is against the law!"
He gave his nodding friends a furtive glance
To make sure they were with him! What he saw
Gave courage to his spirit, and he said:
"To heal upon the sabbath is a sin!
I saw Him heal this man!" He turned his head
And said to Jesus, "When did You begin
To change the law? And do You not admit
That You were wrong? Or do You disagree?"
The accusation simply could not fit
The One who came to earth to set men free!
The Pharisees all knew it was contrived
To trap a man to make a fatal slip.
Their hopes for easy victory revived!
The cry of "Guilty!" waited on each lip!
But Jesus said, "It's lawful to eat food
Upon the sabbath or on any day,
And so it's just as lawful to do good.
Would you have had Me send this man away?
Would you attempt to blind the eyes of all
By kicking up the dust of evil lies,

Hoping that God would fail to hear the call?
He hears when every new-born baby cries!"

What have we got to live for, you and I?
There are so many blessings! For a start—
God's quick reaction to each pleading cry,
His healing strength which lives in every heart!

The threat of evil in the world today
Hangs like a cloud above each human being,
Confounding those who seek to lead the way
Until believing is no longer seeing
And things of value are no longer worth
The effort to protect at any cost,
As everywhere we go around the earth
We hear the cry that everything is lost!
So find a way to save face if you can
And try to save your worldly treasures, too,
So you can buy the image of a man
And plant it in the graveyard when you're through!
The Communists are slowly, surely winning,
And man without a God leaps to success,
Sending the panic-button wildly spinning
And making use of freedom of the press
To brainwash every reader who'll believe it
Simply because the words are holding still—

Believing there is nothing to relieve it,
And lose the precious freedom of their will!

If you climb in a hole and close the cover,
The darkness is appalling and complete!
But just outside, the light will always hover
To help you reach to victory from defeat!
Reach out your hand and touch the hand of Jesus,
And He will grasp and hold you where you stand;
For even in the darkest hole God sees us—
No matter what we've done, He'll understand!
He'll lift you from the nighttime to the day
Which lights His every thought, His every deed!
He'll set your footsteps back upon the way
And give you all the courage that you need
To face the fight of falsehood against truth
And twist the godless arms until they cry
And blame the whole deceit upon their youth
And take what pardon other lies will buy!
As God forgives *us*, so *we* must forgive,
Until we have no foes, but only friends!
Love them until *they* love, and then let live
Until all doubt, all greed, all hatred ends!
This is the way we'll ultimately win,
No matter how the newscast makes it look!
If we believe in God, then let's begin

To take some pages out of His own Book,
For there we'll find the wisdom and the strength
To do the things we always should be doing.
Don't judge a sermon merely by its length—
Remember how long God has been pursuing
And never giving up on you and me,
But hoping against hope that time will tell
And open up our eyes that we may see
Those precious things that God will never sell!
God *gives* through Jesus Christ! And as He gives
We *take*—and look upon this as our right!
And so it is—if each one truly lives
A life of love and tries with all his might
To do the things the Lord would have him do,
Then Communism never will succeed!
We'll kill the lies with everything that's true,
Knowing that God will fill our every need!

How blind! How very blind the human soul!
It digs its very own convenient hole
In which to hide and let the spirit seek
To light the dark within. If it should speak
And try to give some utterance to its thought,
It might well find the freedom which was bought
And paid for on a hill well-named "The Skull,"

No longer bright, but dark and drab and dull,
Well-wrapped against the faintest crack of light
That might leak through—and in the deep of night
Bring a new dawn to brighten each new day
With light and love and truth along the way.
Open your hearts and let the light come in,
That love and true forgiveness may begin!

What have we got to live for, you and I?—
One who knows how to love and to forgive,
A Friend who did not hesitate to die
Upon a cross that you and I might live!

One of the things that plagues us as we go
Along the twisting, turning road of life,
In spite of all the things we think we know
To help us handle any kind of strife,
Is how to face the final call of death!
Unfortunately, we have no control
Of what may bring about our final breath—
Anticipation takes a dreadful toll!
While we are breathing in and breathing out,
While we are walking out and walking in,
We seldom let the shadow of a doubt
Deter a single plan. If we begin
A new idea for something in the future,

We marshal all our energies behind it
And never let a scalpel or a suture
Be more than temporary chains that bind it
And just postpone it for a day or two
Until we get the second wind we need
To run the race and really see it through
Across the finish line. We rarely heed
The kind advice of relatives and friends
Who try to make us take a good, long rest,
Before we learn our future life depends
On doing, not our utmost, but our best.
No matter what we build or where we climb,
No matter how wrong it may seem to some,
Each member of the human race, in time,
Owes God a death, however it may come!
Some day in the middle of a laugh
I hope He summons me! I know I'll feel
The comfort of His precious rod and staff
Wherever I may be! And if I kneel
Before His presence, asking for His love,
I know I'll get forgiveness for my sins
Before I feel His warm and gentle shove
Into the greater life. As it begins
I know I'll know that every mystery
That used to deepen, now will open wide,

And all the things I never used to see
Will stand before me with no place to hide.
I know I'll hear the very smallest sound
And feel it grow into a symphony,
While everywhere above and all around
Each thought will be in perfect harmony!

What have we got to live for, you and I?
It's not enough to know God will forgive?
Well, what about the fact that when we die,
That is the time we'll really start to live!

When Solomon's temple had its dedication,
In all Jerusalem there was an air
Of gay festivity. Throughout the nation
The King had summoned everybody there!
It was a not-to-be-forgotten day.
It was a long-to-be-remembered thing.
So naturally everyone was gay
And did their very best to please the King!
Of course there were the customary few
Who grumbled in the background at the cost.
But they were merely diehards, and they knew
Before they even started they had lost.
The temple was a thing of matchless beauty,
And everyone who saw it knew full well

That Solomon had only done his duty
And in this place the Lord would surely dwell!
The Ark of the Covenant would be within—
The hopes of every man would be inside!
And Solomon said, if any man should sin
Against his neighbor or if he defied
The laws of God, the temple would be there
For each to come and call upon God's name
And ask forgiveness in a secret prayer.
No matter who he was or whence he came,
God would hear and God would always know
If anything he said was not sincere.
If anything he swore to was not so,
He might well lose the things he held most dear.
Deep in the inner darkness of this place
The Lord had told the King that He would dwell,
Where He could look each person in the face
And see those things some of us would not tell!

Within the inmost beings of us all
We find the selfsame darkness, where we keep
The pride, the fear, the things that make us fall,
The self-concern that will not let us sleep;
The greed, the guilt, the envy, and the shame,
The lies and all the little things that hurt,

94

The thoughts to which we dare not give a name,
The hard uncompromising things, the dirt!
But God comes there to meet us, and the dark
Within our souls becomes the brightest light,
Which magnifies the very smallest mark
And brings the sunshine to the dark of night!
But only you can open up that part
Of your own special temple—only you!
And only then can God dwell in your heart,
Becoming part of everything you do!

What have we got to live for, you and I?—
A God whom we can come to without fear!
A God who promises we'll never die!
A God who makes all darkness disappear!

Some warm and magic moment in your life
May make your every thought a treasured dream—
May touch each thought of bitterness or strife
With kindness in a never-ending stream;
And in that magic moment you may see
A total Stranger in a crowded room . . .
And though you do not know Him there may be
Those threads which weave their way across a loom
And make a hidden meaning come to light,

Giving your soul a lift, your heart a beat—
Giving your tired eyes a keener sight
And making your unfinished prayers complete.
Move willingly and quickly to His side!
Tell Him you're not a stranger, but a friend!
Tell Him you'll preach the good news far and wide!
Tell Him your love for Him will never end!

In some magic moment you may find
A Stranger on a quiet, empty street.
He may be poor and dirty, maybe blind—
He may not be the type you like to meet—
But He may need your help! Too many others
May well have passed by on the other side!
Show Him you are one of many brothers—
Open your heart and take Him deep inside!

In some magic moment you may see
A Stranger standing by an empty tomb
Just risen from the dead, and He may be
The One who came to love you! Give Him room
Within your busy life, and let Him see
That your whole heart is His, and let Him know
That you know that His love will set you free,
And that your love will never let Him go!